WORKHOUSE TALES

True Stories of the Victorian Poor Law.

ERIC JENKINS

1998

CORDELIA

ISBN: 0 9522481 1 5
Workhouse Tales: published in Great Britain 1998
by Cordelia (Eric Jenkins)
60 Newton Road, Rushden, Northamptonshire NN10 0HQ.

Catalogue Headings:
Poor Law;
Workhouses;
Northamptonshire;
Victorian.

Also by Eric Jenkins:
Victorian Northamptonshire: the Early Years.

Printed by: Allison Printers, Thrift Street, Wollaston, Northants.

EXPLANATION

The workhouse was, for a century, a phase in the relief of poverty. You will find on the pages that follow, the story of poor relief, demonstrating why and how the workhouse became the universal repository for the destitute. Many parishes had small workhouses until the mid-1830s, operating independently. Most of those buildings have disappeared. The large union workhouses came into existence after 1834, one serving each district. The original intention was that any families or individuals unable to provide for themselves would be obliged to go into the workhouse, rather than claim financial support. Until well into the twentieth century the "bastilles", so called, had the joint-functions of providing sustenance to the poor, and deterring them from requesting it.

The story of the relief of poverty, on the introductory pages, is part of our national history. The individual tales come mainly from one typical county, Northamptonshire. They are intended to show what life in the workhouse was like, and to demonstrate what people, inside and outside, thought of them. They are also intended to give satisfaction to those who wish to know more about the human problems of earlier times.

Sources are listed at the end of the text. The origin of some unidentified items is not known. Those who wish to know more will find the minutes of Boards of Guardians in the County Record Office, and regular comments in the contemporary press.

1. Always With Us

Poverty has always been a social problem, because the factors that create it are ever-present. There will always be families and individuals whose standard of living compares unfavourably with that of their neighbours. There have always been orphans, disabled people, the aged, cases unable to provide adequately for themselves. The altruistic characteristic of the human race has given impetus to schemes of relieving poverty.

Possibly the earliest surviving reference to poverty is in an Assize roll, court records, of 1203. A Titchmarsh man and his mother claimed that they had been unjustly deprived of some land. Their claim was judged to be false, and they were fined; but they were excused payment because they were "paupers". *(1)*

Throughout the Middle Ages, it was normal to expect the Church, through its various religious orders, to relieve the poor. A violent early instance of this expectation is recorded in the following letter of *circa* 1220 from the Constable of Northampton Castle to the Justiciar of England:

"To his dearest lord and friend, Lord Hubert de Burgh, Justiciar of all England, Falkes de Breautt sends greeting and love. I beg to inform you that on St. John the Baptist's Day at the Hospital of St. John, Northampton, a certain accident happened - to wit that when Christ's poor were gathered together at the said Hospital for the receiving of alms, at the entrance to a certain gate a considerable number of the said poor people were thrown down by the rush of those entering, and crushed to death, and many others were wounded and slain by the blows of the vergers.

To explain which more fully I am sending to you Wm. Tilly, Mayor of Northampton, and beg you to consider the matter carefully and to signify to me by your letters what you think might be done in the matter.

Farewell. And as I have not my seal with me I have sealed this letter with my private seal." *(2)*

St. John's Hospital was one of over twenty religious houses in Northampton. One of its buildings still survives. The names of others still exist: Grey Friars is the name of the 'bus station that stands on the site of the monastic house of that Order.

In the county, there were many monastic establishments, ranging in size from the huge monastery at Pipewell to tiny residential houses attached to many of the parish churches. All of them provided assistance to the needy.

The question of financing arises. The religious houses were rich, and constantly growing richer. Giving aid to the poor caused no strain on monastic resources. They were in regular receipt of bequests. Any rich man making his will was likely to include a legacy for a local monastery. Why? Because it could ensure a place in Heaven. The contents of monastic coffers greatly increased as a result of the Crusades. Rich men feeling the urge to drive the Turks from the Holy Land, as the Pope directed, left their property in the care of the monks. Many crusaders failed to return, and their possessions became permanent assets of monasteries.

2. Beggars Coming to Town.

The status of the poor was seriously undermined in two ways during the reign of Henry VIII. First, the enclosure movement gained momentum. English wool was in demand on the Continent, and sheep became big business. Landowners were changing the arable land of the old open fields into enclosed pasture, so depriving many families of their traditional right to cultivate. Result: families unable to produce their own food. Secondly, Henry's determination to replace the Queen with one who could produce a male heir, led to the break with the Church of Rome. The new Anglican Church had the King as its Head, and rules to suit him, but the monks and nuns still belonged to the old Church. That meant that thousands of opponents would be able to use their considerable influence against him. During the 1530s the monasteries were closed, and their estates taken into the King's hands. Result: no religious houses to perform the function of welfare and relief for the poor. By the mid-sixteenth century, enclosures had put many poor people on the roads; and the monastic houses that previously would have provided for them, were closed. Wandering bands of beggars on the highway became a pressing social problem. The pathetic, frail type of mendicant was not typical. "Sturdy beggars" and vagabonds were a danger to legitimate travellers, and a problem in towns when gangs of them invaded.

Tudor legislation intended to deal with these problems, failed. Instructions to change enclosed land back to open arable were simply ignored and never enforced. A number of measures to deal with poverty also failed. The threat of flogging and branding did not deter vagabonds; and "houses of correction" were a soft option.

In Northamptonshire in 1571, justices ordered the parish constables to round up all vagabonds. *(3)* After watching for a day and a night, they apprehended eight, including three women. They were held in the stocks at Polebrook and Bulwick, stripped to the waist, publicly whipped, and sent out of the county.

Brackley was troubled by vagabonds entering the county from the south. The Corporation employed a "beggar-banger", an official whose duty was to expel them from the town. *(4)*

In 1585, the Northampton Assembly (Town Council) decided to give 21 poor people a badge each, to authorise them to beg at the town inns. Why 21? Seven beggars at a time were allowed to operate for two weekdays. Any beggars caught in Northampton without a badge were to be locked up. *(5)*

Also in 1585, the Jesus Hospital was founded at Rothwell by Owen Ragsdale, a philanthropist who had inherited much property. It was to house poor old men of the district. At Higham Ferrers there had been a similar foundation, the Bede House, since 1423. St. John's Hospital, at Northampton, had survived the dissolution of the monasteries, because it had a special constitution by which its purpose was the relief of the poor. For ten years, however, it had supported an absentee Master, living in Jersey, and as a result of mismanagement "the said Hospitall was greatly decayed". *(6)* Income was not being used for its intended purpose. "Hardly the xxth parte [was] given to the reliefe of any impotent aged or feeble persons."

Written records of income had been burnt by the orders of the Master. Prominent townsmen complained to the Privy Council, but no action was taken, and the Mastership continued to be a "lucrative sinecure" for another century.

Wellingborough Union Workhouse (later Isebrook Hospital).

3. On the Parish.

Elizabeth's Parliament made a final attempt to solve the problem of poverty, two years before the Tudor period came to an end with her death. The 1601 Poor Law declared the parish to be the proper unit to deal with poverty. All those deserving poor relief could claim it - in their native parishes. Every parish was to have an overseer empowered to collect financial contributions and provide relief to the poor, so long as they had been born there. This law was very important, not just because it worked successfully for two centuries, and cleared the bands of vagabonds from the highways. It initiated the system of local taxes for local services, and it brought into existence the world's first state welfare.

Methods of relieving poverty varied. Dole payments were made; loaves of bread were given out; medical treatment was authorised; apprenticeships were arranged.

Compulsory attendance at Church on Sundays was, at that time, enforced by law, and so it was convenient for Poor Law business to be conducted before or after service. Shelving with loafsize divisions still exists in some parish churches, and in one instance, the oven in which the bread was baked is to be seen near the altar. Parishes were encouraged to provide work for the poor, and small workhouses were eventually provided in larger communities. At Northampton, the inmates were set to grinding malt. Charity boards surviving in many parish churches bear witness to local benefactors who bequeathed property or left investments, the profits of which were intended to defray the cost of poor relief, pay the cost of apprenticeships, or provide almshouses. The parish system worked smoothly until the end of the Napoleonic Wars. A quarter of a century of war brought economic and social problems. Britain's pre-war trading partners had made other arrangements and were unlikely to resume their former business with us. Our new Corn Law, blocking grain imports, discouraged other countries from trading with us. At the same time, soldiers and sailors were coming home expecting to resume their former employment.

"What a melancholy event happened yesterday at Northampton", wrote the Vicar of Earls Barton on 1st December 1815. "...Two more families have been sent to us by lawful authority... I have not a house or even a room to receive them"(7) In May 1817, he wrote: "Our Poor Rates are so extremely high that I know not how we shall be able to pay them..." A farmer's widow at Pytchley paid three instalments of £16 10s for the Poor Rate between 26th January and 11th June 1816. Her groceries cost less than £10. (8) Parish relief was under great pressure. A scheme of relief called Speenhamland had been adopted in many parishes. Its name came from the Berkshire parish where it originated. Magistrates at intervals decided a minimum wage, related to the curent price of bread. Any man with an income lower than the agreed basic rate, was eligible to claim the difference in poor relief. It had good and bad points. No family had to exist on less than the minimum wage, and it was easy to administer; but the workshy had their earnings made up; and mean employers could underpay, knowing that the parish would subsidise. Overseers also used a practice called "roundsmen". The unemployed were taken round the local farms and other work-places and offered as cheap labour. Obviously intended to relieve the pressure on the poor rate, it often had the opposite effect, because some farmers preferred parish labour, and their regular workers became unemployed and, yes, went on parish relief.

The requirement that the poor should have relief only from their native parishes, caused many arguments.   Two

Northampton Union Workhouse (later St. Edmund's Hospital).

curious letters contain examples of long-distance claims. The first was written to the Rushden Overseers, probably in 1824:

"i am sorry to inform you through want of trade and illness i am reduced to want and unless you will immediately releive me something i must go to the parish i am in for i am under the docter hands... i would trouble your parish gentlemen you must do as you think proper

Whether me and my Family are to come to the parish or you will send me some money to carry on my business... from your Humble Servant, Thos. Darnell Vine Court, White Chapple Road" *(9)*

The second also from London, was received by the Earls Barton Overseers in December 1833:

"Gentlemen, I Have the Missfortune to inform you that my Husband Joseph Tibbett is now under Sentence of death in the Cells of Newgate for he has the Missfortune to be connected with a sett of House breakers wich are all Taken and Condemd I have applied to the Parish for Relief and they will do nothing for me... I am now makeing Shift at a friends house with my Famely five Children untill such Times that I Here from you Gentlemen I am in The greatest of distress and Unless you advance me Sufficente to pay up... Gentlemen I shall wait for an Answer to this letter for a Short Time wich I Hope you will Answer as soon as you can, or I must be oblidged to come down with my family for I Cannot much Longer Subsist without Releif. Please to direct me at 29 Loyd Row near Sadlers Wells London. Mary Tibbett" *(10)*

In both these cases, the dilemma of the overseers was whether the money demanded should be sent, or the risk taken of having large families descend on them, to be permanently on relief.

No doubt a similar situation led to the following sad story of 1829. *(11)*

"...Inquest was held at the New Inn, Hackleton, on the body of a poor woman apparently between 40 and 50 years old, of the name of Mary Ann Gowers, who was found dead on the preceding day in the Leicester wagon when passing through the above place. Verdict - Died by the visitation of God. It appeared from the evidence of a very respectable young woman who had travelled with the deceased, that about ten o'clock on Saturday night, she was placed in the wagon by some ruthless person at Leicester to be conveyed to her parish of Plumstead, Kent - that she in a state of great pain and weakness, and two men had some difficulty in lifting her up the ladder, as she was incapable of supporting herself; and that one of them, together with several of the spectators, hearing her groaning, and seeing her condition, indignantly called out 'Shame'. She was incapable of conversing at any time on the journey but continued groaning. When the wagon stopped at Hackleton the vital spark was totally extinct".

4. Investigating Poor Relief 1832-34.

A Whig Government under Earl Grey, elected in 1832, set about reforming factories, the slave trade, education, the law, and even Parliament itself. To investigate the working of the Poor Law, a Royal Commission was set up. Every parish was required to answer a questionnaire, and to follow this up, each county was visited by an assistant commissioner (inspector) who made his own observations.

The thirty-six questions were directed to the parish overseer, but were usually answered by the clergyman. They began predictably and innocuously with requests for details of parish farming: acreage, land-use, labour, wages, seasonal work. There were questions about housing, tenants and their rent. Then came the questions on poor relief, somewhat tendentious. "Have you a workhouse? What number of individuals received relief last week, not being in the workhouse? Have you any able-bodied labourers in employment, receiving an allowance or regular relief from your parish, for themselves or for their families? Say whether the system of roundsmen is practised."

Joseph John Richardson was the Assistant Commissioner who visited and reported on Northamptonshire. *(12)* His twenty-page report had many complaints about the various styles of parish relief. He was scathing about the following observations:

1. Payments of relief to the able-bodied.

2. Allowances to any one who was employed for any part of a week (the Speenhamland system).

3. No proper "parish" work for claimants.

4. Insufficient investigation of claims.

5. Lack of discipline.

6. Early marriage (because it meant more children for young parents to feed).

7. Paying "distant" paupers to stay away.

8. False economy. (Doctors' fees too low, so that the sick poor were not treated, causing more to pay out on funerals, and longterm maintenance).

9. Expensive law suits to resettle paupers in their own parishes, when "discipline" would make them go of their own accord.

10. Chasing runaway fathers of bastard children. (They discharged their debts by a short term in prison; or married the mothers and thus took even more parish money).

Was there anything at all that Richardson admired? Oh, yes.

He strongly approved of the village where paupers were all made to work stone-quarrying. (Very few claims, there!). He liked paid emigration. There were quite a number of individuals and families whose passages on emigrant ships to the U.S.A., Canada or Australia, had been paid by their parishes. He admired parishes that gave allotments of land - but with no further payments of relief.

Richardson made observations about two of the bigger parish workhouses. In Northampton, he "went down to the workhouse of All Saints, which was, as I had expected, very comfortable, so much so, that the inmates, old and young, were allowed bread and meat five days in a week, and the only work was sweeping in the streets, which was done in the usual idle style; it was capable of containing 70 people; there were about 40 when I visited it, 12 women (one or two of whom had come there to be delivered of bastard children), eight children, and about 20 men, most of whom were old, crippled or idiotic. There was a separation between the sexes, and a difference made in the treatment of the impotent and the able-bodied, but every man in the house was allowed threepence a week for tobacco, and a pint of beer a day, and the expenses of the workhouse amounted, during the last year, to £433. The notion of making the workhouse a place of discipline, seemed never to have occurred to any one, the object being rather, as they told me, to make the poor comfortable. I do not consider the putting those who would not conform to the rules of the house into a cell occasionally, to be an exception, as the rules themselves are too lenient. It will not be deemed astonishing that the rates in this parish do not decrease..."

He also went into the workhouse at Peterborough, which he considered to be worse managed than that at All Saints. "Out of 46 inmates, there were not less than seven able-bodied men, and several stout boys, who were better fed, on bacon four times a week, in the workhouse than their honest exertions out of it would have enabled them to be. There was no separation between the sexes except at night, nor [between] the different classes of poor, nor any difference of treatment. The consequence naturally, is that persons who have once wintered in the workhouse, come there again the next year, to stay two or three months at a time. The Master of the workhouse farms the poor at two shillings 10d a head per week, having the benefit of their labour in a small farm at a little distance, or in weaving and beating hemp at home, and giving them a little tobacco money by way of encouragement to work. They are, of course, as lazy as possible."

Kettering Union Workhouse (later St. Mary's Hospital)

5. A New Poor Law, 1834.

Ministers of the Whig Government had been greatly influenced by an admired political philosopher, Jeremy Bentham. For over fifty years, Bentham had published pamphlets advocating a particular style of government to modernize Britain. He was in favour of centralising the administration of public services. "Utilitarianism" became the watchword of trendy politicians. Efficiency should replace sentiment. Traditional methods must be replaced by new schemes designed to bring "the greatest good for the greatest number". Bentham died in 1832. (In accordance with his dying wish, he was never buried, and his body is still sitting in his favourite chair). His death gave impetus to his ideas, and the report of the Poor Law Commission was strongly utilitarian. The greatest number were NOT the poor! The Benthamites in the Government would inevitably bring forward legislation of which their mentor would approve.

The new law was The Poor Law Amendment Act (4 and 5 William IV, c.76). First, the centralisation: "I. Be it therefore enacted... to appoint three fit Commissioners to carry this Act into execution. II That the said Commissioners shall... sit as a Board... XV. That the administration of relief to the poor throughout England and Wales... shall be subject to the direction and control of the said Commissioners..."

Parish relief ended. In every district, the parishes were grouped into "unions". Every union was to be directed by a board of elected "guardians". Overseers were to take their instructions from the guardians. "It shall not be lawful for any overseer to give further relief than such as shall be ordered by such guardians".

Every union was to build a workhouse. The Report of the Commission had firmly suggested that no relief should be given unless the recipient was inside the workhouse, but that was not quite realistic. There would always be circumstances of hardship, perhaps a medical condition, which would make outdoor relief essential. (Outdoor relief was assistance given while the claimant was outside the workhouse, probably still at home).

Conditions in the workhouse were intended to be "less eligible" than the normal living conditions of a self-supporting labourer.

A person needing assistance should be discouraged from asking for it. If assistance meant workhouse, it would be the last resort. Workhouse accommodation was far from sufficient. 350 big new ones needed to be built. The Central Poor Law Board gave advice, recommended plans, and issued instructions as to how they should be run when they were built. To pay for their new union workhouses, the guardians were permitted to sell off any property previously owned by their parishes. That meant goodbye to many tracts of land hitherto regarded as common land, and parish workhouses became private property.

6. In and Out of the Workhouse

A SURPRISE IN THE OLD HOUSE

In 1835, the Brixworth Union was formed, and the board of guardians arranged for a big new union workhouse to be built. Meanwhile, they continued to use some of the small old parish workhouses. One of them was at Moulton.

Some years previously, an old woman of Moulton had become an inmate, and she took in with her everything she owned - an old bedstead and a trunk. When she died, the parish overseer went to her nearest relatives to ask for the cost of her funeral. They refused to pay, and the parish retained the bedstead and trunk.

When the new Brixworth workhouse was ready, the Union abandoned the old workhouse at Moulton. A public auction of the contents was held on 7th July 1837. The bedstead and trunk parted company. The trunk went for two shillings, but two buyers claimed it, and it was put up for bids again. It was knocked down for two shillings and ninepence (15p) to a Moulton woman. Her husband, a labourer, seemed amused by his wife's purchase, and began to examine the old trunk. Soon he began to strip off the grimy paper with which it was covered. His wife remonstrated with him: "You're spoiling it". He had heard of secret drawers in ancient trunks, and persisted in his exploration. Sure enough, as he peeled one side, he uncovered a sunken drawer. It was tightly packed with gold coins. There were over a hundred, dating from all the Stuart kings. *(13)*

WHAT DID THEY WEAR?

As the new union workhouses neared completion, the guardians invited tenders for the supply of clothing. From their advertisements, we are able to know what was worn in the workhouse.

At Kettering, men wore dark brown suits with waistcoats, grey worsted stockings, strong shoes and "hightops", and coarse felt hats. Women and girls were in striped cotton gowns, black worsted stockings, blue spotted handkerchiefs, aprons of strong coarse cloth, cotton shawls and jean stays. Boys were clothed distinctly from the men, in fustian jackets and trousers, and Scotch worsted caps.

At Brackley, men were in drab fustian jackets and waistcoats, but the old men were different in drab woollen coats, waistcoats and trousers. All wore worsted stockings, cotton neck-cloths and white thrashers' hats, though the boy's version was covered with oilskin. The name almost certainly refers to the style worn by farm-labourers whilst threshing. By 1842, male headgear had changed to black glazed hats, and for boys, Scoth caps. Women's and girls' clothing was evidently made on the premises, from a variety of materials: stout flannel, unbleached calico, checked muslin, linsey wolsey, blue and white speckled chambrey, white serge, mulberry serge, mixed linen and cotton check. Stays, worsted stockings and neckerchiefs were purchased for them.

At Daventry, women were in straw bonnets, black worsted hose, and blue checked cotton kerchiefs. Men wore cotton cord, Kilmarnock caps, and grey worsted stockings. Boys had smockfrocks over fustian suits, with worsted caps.

Beavertreen suits were worn at Thrapston by all males. Footwear was grey worsted stockings and strong low shoes, the boys' version being nailed. Females wore blue and white print gowns, check muslin caps, check linen aprons, blue and white neckerchiefs, black worsted hose and low shoes.

For a final example, look at Brixworth inmates in 1843. The men attired in light fustian suits, the women in drabbett frocks, all in blue or yellow neckerchiefs. Footwear was strong ankle shoes, sprigged for women; for both boys and girls, half-boots - nailed for boys and sprigged for girls. Infants under three were provided with their own shoes.

WHAT DID THEY EAT?

Similar advertisements inviting tenders for the supply foodstuffs to the union workhouses tell us what the inmates ate. The standard unit of bread was the quartern loaf (to weigh four pounds). Wellingborough Guardians wanted it made of "good seconds flour". Loose flour was "best seconds". Meat was "rounds and rands of good fat beef... buttocks, clods and stickings of beef off the bone; forequarters of good mutton; good salt butter, good thin cheese, good moist sugar, good white peas, and new milk; best seconds wheaten flour, good black tea, black pepper, oatmeal, good patna rice.

Brackley required similar supplies, plus "rounds and whites of beef with shins cut off at the joints... and suet".

At Daventry, the "good two meal cheese" was specified. There, notably, "good sound port wine" was ordered, as well as ale, beer and liquors". The advertisement (March 1841) did say that the alcohol was "for the sick inmates in the Workhouse".

The provision of ale and beer is not really surprising. Many ordinary families drank their own beer rather than beverages like tea or coffee, which were much more expensive. The Temperance Movement was in its infancy, and it was not yet necessary to be licensed to sell alcohol. As time passed and public opinion divided on "the demon drink", the provision of beer to workhouse inmates depended on the attitude of the guardians in each union.

The following diet for men was recommended by the Central Poor Law Board. *(14)* Breakfasts: 6 oz. bread and 1½ oz. cheese; Dinners [mid-day], Sunday, Tuesday and Thursday: 5 oz. meat and ½lb. potatoes, Monday, Wednesday, Friday, Saturday: 1½ pints soup; Supper, days on which there was meat for dinner, 6 oz. bread and 1½ pints broth; Supper on other days, 6 oz. bread and 2 oz. cheese. There was an alternative diet. Breakfasts: 6 oz. bread and 1 oz. cheese. Dinners, Sunday: 16 oz. meat pudding plus vegetables; Monday, Wednesday, Thursday and Saturday: 7 oz. bread and 1 oz. cheese; Tuesday and Friday: 16 oz. suet pudding plus vegetables. Supper: 6 oz. bread and 1 oz. cheese.

LOOKING FOR A SCANDAL, AND FINDING ONE

The new Poor Law was a matter of political controversy. It was Whig Party legislation intended to solve a problem that had grown during long years of Tory administration. Understandably, the Tories would wish to find fault with it. No political advantage was to be gained by siding with the people experiencing the anxieties and discomforts of the new system, because they belonged to a class which did not yet have the right to vote in elections. More was to be gained by exposing scandals - mismanagement, cruelty, incidents that would incur the disgust of the voters.

In Northampton, the first workhouse topic to cause bitterness was the appointment of a chaplain. He happened to be a Curate at All Saints' Church in that town. In a district where Nonconformity was strong, an Anglican appointment, with a salary of £50 per annum, was bound to draw fire. That sum, said a hostile handbill, would maintain eight paupers. "Ought he to wear workhouse dress, if he is taking your money?"

The first to die in a Northamptonshire union workhouse was a new baby at Brackley, and infant mortality was too common for that to attract attention. When a man over 80 was found dead in his bed at the same workhouse, the Guardians and the Master were instantly on the defensive. An inquest was held, and "the Coroner was induced to request the jury to examine the witnesses closely, for the satisfaction of the public as well as themselves".(15) When the Master, John Sumpter, said in evidence that the old man had seemed normal on the night before his death, and had eaten his allowance - ten ounces of bread and one ounce of cheese - the Coroner ordered the supper allowance to brought in for the jury to see. They all considered it to be "sufficient for any man" and rather more than any of them would have eaten. Inmates were brought in to say that they were very comfortable and had no complaints. The jury were taken to the workhouse and told to question the paupers. Another old man, well known to all the jurymen, was quoted: "Why, we have plenty of food, plenty of clothes, and a good bed to sleep on. What more can we desire?" The unanimous verdict was "Death by the Visitation of God".

Two-and-a-half years later, another death in the same workhouse was the subject of a six-hour inquest. A seven-yearold boy, William Hirons, had been scalded to death when hot water was thrown over him as he sat in a bath-tub. There was now another Master, Howe, and he had been concerned in the incident. The jury returned a verdict of "Accidental Death" but requested the Coroner to caution the Master about future care. Soon afterwards Howe moved to another mastership at Eton Workhouse.

This incident was brought back before public notice in February 1841, when Howe was dismissed from Eton, and fined £10, for ill-treating a female inmate. She was a young mother, and he had denied her access to her sick child, and locked her in a small room in winter for over thirty hours, without heat, food, adequate clothing, and no "chamber utensil".

The Brackley Guardians commenced a public argument among themselves, in the columns of The Times, over what had really happened to the boy Hirons, the previous June. Information had been withheld from the inquest, and even from some of the Guardians. At their meeting two days after the inquest, it had been proposed that Howe be dismissed. They discussed his conduct, his lack of humanity, his treatment of all inmates, and questioned his integrity. Possibly because it might reflect on their own competence, they decided to reprimand Howe rather than dismiss him. The Chairman, in his letter to the Times, insisted that Howe had not been dismissed, but had resigned; that there was a background of bad relations between the Master and some of the Guardians; and that accusations of misbehaviour were unsubstantiated. Finally, it was revealed by a local clergyman, that the boy's mother had been pressurised into withholding evidence from the Guardians, and from the Inquest.

In the meantime, at Daventry Union Workhouse, a two-year old toddler had fallen through the seat of the women's privy, and suffocated. That did not cause a scandal.

PETTY CRIME AT THE WORKHOUSE

The Report on the Northampton County Gaol for the years 1840 and 1841, by the Inspector of Prisons (16) included a section that the other prison reports did not have. There was a list of twenty-three persons sent to prison from the Union Workhouses. It gave their names, ages, offences and sentences. Some of them were imprisoned simply for "misbehaviour"; several for "carrying away clothing". Two teenagers from Brixworth Workhouse served 14 days for "wasting 8 oz. of coir".

The magistrates at Quarter Sessions in January 1843, having perused this document, queried the case of a 16-year-old girl from Kettering Workhouse, sentenced to 21 days for "wasting soap". It was explained to them that she had taken the soap to Kettering Market Square and tried to sell it. She had a record of "lewd behaviour".

"Carrying away clothing" usually meant discharging themselves from the House and failing to hand in their Workhouse clothes. An 1838 advertisement gives an example:

"KETTERING UNION

ABSCONDED from the Kettering Workhouse, with the Union clothing, on Sunday, under the pretence of attending public worship, JOSEPH ROWLATT, of the parish of Kettering. [He] is nearly blind, about 55 years old, walks erect, with a long stick. Height, 5 ft. 8 in., dark complexion, grey hair, and rather stout made. He had on, when he left, the workhouse dress, consisting of a dark brown cloth coat, waistcoat, and trousers, nearly new. Whoever will apprehend and bring [him] to the Union Workhouse, at Kettering, shall receive a reward of ONE SOVEREIGN, on application to the Master..." *(17)*

In March 1841, Northampton Magistrates sent two men to the Borough Gaol (not the County Gaol in the Report referred to above). They had left their allotted tasks in the Workhouse on the previous Wednesday and Thursday. Those two days just happened to be the days of the Northampton Races!

A frequent offence brought before Petty Sessions Courts was leaving wives and children "chargeable to the parish". That meant families left in the Workhouse, while the nominal breadwinner was away on the loose. The Wollaston Relieving Officer took Joseph Baker before Wellingborough Magistrates in 1844, charged with leaving his wife and child, there being £7 chargeable to Rushden. (Wollaston and Rushden were within the Wellingborough Union, and the family were in that Workhouse. Baker was actually a Coventry man).

The police superintendent, standing behind Baker, told the Bench: "The defendant was committed to prison some time back, for felony." Baker turned round sharply and said: "Bad luck to you, and the measles! Haven't I paid her Majesty in full, and got the receipt for it? And I ain't sure she didn't say Thank you, Joseph. And, you know, my dear fellow, such information as yours is only calculated to give the magistrates a bad opinion of me".

The Chairman interrupted: "Are you going to pay the £7? Unless you pay you will go to prison for three months".

Baker: It's worse than Coventry!

Chairman: Three months.

A vagrant named Mason was taken into the Thrapston Workhouse on a December night in 1868. During the night, he burnt his own clothing. Next morning, the Master provided him with a pair of trousers and set him to work. Mason decided to leave immediately, and set off towards Oundle, tearing off his workhouse trousers on the way. In Oundle, in a state of nudity, he set about breaking plate glass shop windows. He was surrounded by Oundle townsmen carrying whips and escorted to the police station. At Oundle Petty Sessions he was sent to prison for one month.

A CHANGE OF SCHOOLMASTER

A boy aged eight, from Northampton Workhouse, undressed in Court at Northampton Petty Sessions in August 1843. The magistrates saw livid red wheals from shoulder to hip, and there was severe bruising on the boy's head. William Emery, the Schoolmaster at the Union Workhouse, stood charged with brutally beating him. Asked to explain, he said: "The boy is of an unruly disposition. I have had great difficulty in managing him." He did express contrition, and told the Court that he had not realised that he had inflicted such severe punishment on the child.

Emery was asked to comment on the report that the

offence which had led to the beating was that the boy insisted on saying "Dod" for "God".

"That's not true", replied Emery. "The boy insisted on saying t-h-e-n spelt "ours".

The schoolmaster was ordered to pay a fine of £2. Several of the Northampton Guardians were present in Court, and after their next meeting, advertisements were put out for a new Schoolmaster at the Workhouse.

THE UNEXPECTED DEATH OF ANN FORRESTER

A week before Christmas 1846, Ann Forester was taken into the Workhouse at Northampton as a vagrant. She was not known to any one there, and she said that she had come from Brixworth, a few miles away. She was "in a dirty and diseased state", and the Surgeon, Mr. Woods was asked to look at her. He found nothing of a dangerous nature. Two days later, Mr. Woods was "quite astonished" when he was told that she was dead. For the Coroner, he made a post mortem examination, and told the Inquest that the liver and heart were diseased, and the lungs were one mass of disease. From these and other symptoms, Mr. Woods "had not the slightest doubt whatever that death was occasioned by the drinking of ardent spirits to a great excess".*(18)*

The inquest jury's verdict was "Death From Excessive Drinking".

Ann Forrester was sixteen years old!

AT THE CASUAL WARD IN 1869

The union workhouse had a department at which tramps could be provided with overnight lodging, on condition that they had no money. In Northamptonshire, these wards became controversial in 1869, thanks to the Rev. Francis Litchfield. He was a vociferous Guardian at Brackley, a Magistrate, and an active Tory. Thirty-six years earlier, he had been singled out for praise in the Report of the Poor Law Commission, for his no nonsense methods of organising poor relief in his parish. Now he was concerned about the increase in the number of vagrants lurking in the County. He had counted 342 tramps received into Brackley Workhouse in the last quarter of 1868. In the corresponding quarter of 1867 there had been only 240.

At Quarter Sessions, in April, he lectured his fellow magistrates. "A census of vagrants was made on the 4th of this month. On that day, there were no less than 119 vagrants in this County; and yet there were only 52 vagrants punished in the whole year... There should be an entire change in the casual wards, where these men and women sleep. I do not want to stop charity, but merely to direct it and prevent it being abused... I went, the other day, to three tramp wards. Many magistrates and guardians have never been in them. Imagine a room, the floor covered with straw from end to end, and in a most disgusting state. The master of one said he had been a policeman in London for 18 years, amongst the lowest people; but he had never seen worse scenes nor heard worse language than what is to be seen and heard from the tramps. There is neither ventilation nor separation. I will repeat a conversation I had with a master of one of these places. 'Where do your men sleep at night?' 'Upon the straw.' 'What do they sleep under?' 'Under a rug.' 'What do you do with the rug in the morning?' 'Nothing particular.' 'Do you ever fumigate it?' 'Never.' 'Do you ever wash it?' 'I suppose in the process of time, we do.' 'Do these men ever come into this tramp ward with nits upon them?' 'Continually.' 'With fleas upon them?' 'Oh, yes.' 'Lousy?' 'Yes, to any extent. When I have held up a rug and shaken it, I have seen the lice drop out, twenty or thirty at a time.'

"Gentlemen, I want to propose three things - soap, separation, silence." (Laughter) "If we adopt those three principles, we should do more to drive out such men from the County than by any other means, and still more the women, who could not endure silence." (Laughter)

Within a few days, posters were issued by Litchfield's colleagues at Brackley: "Caution to beggars. Notice is hereby given, that the police have strict orders to apprehend every person found violating the law by begging..."

The first to be apprehended in that district was a dyer from Liverpool, who had his wife and two children with him. He was carrying a bag with bread in it, and he had sixpence-halfpenny in his pocket. He was sentenced to twenty-one days with hard labour, for begging. His wife and children were ordered to make their way home.

The casual ward of Northampton Union Workhouse was called the Mendicity Office. On 30th June, the Mayor, in his magisterial capacity, was in the chair at the Borough Petty Sessions. A man was sent for trial at the Assizes on a charge of arson. As an excuse for his crime, he said that he was hungry. He had slept at the Mendicity Office the previous night, and had received three ounces of bread for supper and the same for breakfast. The magistrates were of the opinion that this was insufficient. The Mayor sent for the Mendicity Officer, Parker, and asked him to comment. "I gave him twice that amount, and I was not bound to give him that, because he had twopence on him. There were eleven cases that night, and I cut up six pounds of bread amongst them. That was at a cost of sevenpence-halfpenny. It is left to my discretion. If I think the case is not a deserving one, I give four ounces only, but I always give a cripple two ounces more."

The Mayor: The man complained that the bread was given to him as if he were a dog.

Parker: On that morning, another man who seemed to be an honest wayfarer, got eight ounces of bread, and I also gave him a cup of coffee. Sometimes I give nothing out at night because frequently tramps come into the Office with great hunches of bread which they have begged from the public.

The Mayor: Did you give this man coffee?

Parker: No, he didn't deserve it.

Mayor: If they are found begging during the day, they are liable to be apprehended, so the amount you give them should be sufficient to support life.

An anonymous citizen the previous autumn, had intercepted the vagrants leaving the Mendicity Office on successive mornings, and taken their bread to be weighed "at a respectable shop". The weights varied between 3¼ and 6¼ ounces. The smallest amount had been given to a woman who had been made to scrub the Office floor before receiving it.

DON'T TRY TOO HARD TO CATCH HER

Selina P. was an inmate of Towcester Union Workhouse, and described then as "an imbecile". Another inmate,

Sarah C. lost patience with her, one day in 1870, and assaulted her. The assault was serious enough to be brought before Towcester Petty Sessions, but by then, Sarah had left. As now, when defendants did not appear in Court to answer the charge, a warrant, was issued for their arrest. The Towcester Magistrates were told that Sarah C. had left the Workouse with her five children.

The prosecuting solicitor said: "I am applying for a warrant for the arrest of Sarah C, but as long as she keeps away, I don't care if it is not executed: it will save the Union a matter of £50 a year."

GUARDIANS DISCUSSING THE LABOUR TEST

"The Labour Test" was the term used for work given to able-bodied workhouse inmates without the option. It was discussed by the Northampton Guardians in January 1871. Picking oakum was separating the strands of old rope to make caulking material for ships. It was a task associated then with work done in prison by convicts at hard labour. The Master of the Workhouse, Brannen, told the Guardians: "There are twenty-six men now in the labour shed, picking oakum in accordance with the labour test. The oakum is bought at sixteen shillings per ton unpicked, and when picked, we can sell it to the firm we bought it from, for one guinea per ton. Each man can pick about four pounds of oakum per day, but the quantity is generally regulated according to the physical capability of the man seeking relief. We found, last year, that the men could easily break the required quantity of stones in about three hours, sometimes, whilst the picking oakum generally occupied the whole day. Picking oakum is harder than breaking stones, and the men dislike it more.

Mason, Guardian: I am inclined to think that the breaking of stones is the more profitable employment - or how is it that men on the roads can earn ten or twelve shillings a week at it?

FitzHugh, Guardian: Sixteen or eighteen shillings a week, some of them.

Mason: I do not see why we should degrade a man to the position of a criminal by requiring him to pick oakum. Let us give a man work by which he can make a profit.

Saull, Guardian: That is mistaken philanthropy.

Markham, Chairman: If you were a pauper, Mr. Mason, would you not rather pick oakum in a shed in this weather, than break stones in a garden? [Seventeen degrees of frost was recorded in Northampton on this day]

Mason: If I were a pauper, I should prefer to do that which was profitable.

Saull: Mr. Mason would be in favour of giving the paupers hot dinners every day, and treating them too well. He is evidently not acquainted with the characters that are fond of coming to the Union. If his plan were adopted, we should be swarmed with people of the idle class. The object of the labour test is to protect the rate-payers.

Mason: If ever I had the misfortune to become a pauper, and were treated as some guardians treat paupers, I should certainly rather be in prison.

Saull: You might. I wouldn't help you.

Master Brannen: Out of 117 cases at the labour test last winter, I could pick out half a dozen deserving cases. Some of them got work directly they left, and after working for a week or so, they left off so that they could go to the races.

SETTING FIRE TO THE WORKHOUSE

On the same day in January 1871 that Northampton Guardians were arguing about picking oakum, David Bushell made an attempt to burn down the Brixworth Union Workhouse. The evidence against him was first heard in the Northampton Petty Sessions. The first witness was Richard Giles, the Master of the Workhouse.

Giles: ...He was admitted to the Workhouse by an order from the Relieving Officer. While I was talking to him at the door, Mr. Harper, the surgeon, came up and told me there was a smell of fire. I told my son, Samuel, to go and see. He returned in a few minutes and said the place was on fire. I turned to Bushell and said, "How did that happen?" I then went to see the fire. A stable was burnt, and part of the female receiving ward had to be broken down to save the main building. There were over a hundred people in the House at the time. Bushell was afterwards taken into custody by the police. He has constantly been in the House during the past few years, and he has, several times, been in prison for assaults on me and others. He has several times threatened to set fire to the Workhouse, and to farm-buildings in the neighbourhood.

Frederick Luther Harper, Surgeon: ...On that evening, about nine o'clock, I was riding from Spratton to Brixworth. Near the Union, I noticed a great smell of burning pine wood, and I saw smoke coming from the stables. I rang the bell, and gave alarm to Mr. Giles. I had previously seen two constables near Spratton Station, and I rode after them.

Police-Sergeant John B. Martin: ...The prisoner had come out of custody on the day before the fire, and I called at the Union about ten minutes before nine, to enquire if he was there. He was not, and I went on down the road towards Spratton Station. On the way, I met P.C. Frost. We heard the Workhouse alarm bell ring, and shortly afterwards we met Mr. Harper, who told us there was a fire. I went down to the village to give the alarm. Afterwards, in consequence of information from P.C. Frost, I went down to examine some footprints leading to and from the field at the back of the Workhouse. There was snow on the ground. They led to the fire. I covered up the footmarks, and afterwards went with the Master and procured the boots which the prisoner had been wearing. They were by his bedside. I compared the boots with the footmarks, and they exactly corresponded. There were no other footmarks. The boots were nailed up in a peculiar manner at the front, and the impressions of the nails were very clear. In my presence, in November last, the prisoner said that he would do something to get himself transported to Australia.

P.C. Jesse Frost: ...I accompanied Sergeant Martin to the fire at about nine o'clock. I noticed footmarks from the corner of the garden to where the fire was. I saw where someone had got over the wall...

Inspector George Williamson gave evidence of the fire damage, the footmarks, and then told about the arrest of Bushell. "He was in bed, and after getting dressed, he went into the porter's room with the Master and myself. After I cautioned him, he said: 'You've got the wrong man then'. I brought him to the lock-up at Northampton. He complained of his knee, and I allowed him to sit by the fire. While sitting there, he said he fell over a wall, and he did set fire to the stable. I again cautioned him, and he repeated what he had said. He said he went up the garden wall to get away, and threw the matches down by the side of the wall. He said he had bought them at East Haddon on the Monday... I made enquiries at East Haddon and found out where he bought the matches...

David Bushell (who was 57 years old) was given the opportunity to address the Court, but declined. He was committed to stand trial at the Assizes.

At Northampton Assizes, he pleaded guilty to the charge. His criminal record was extensive, and Judge Blackburn sentenced him to five years penal servitude, expressing regret that he could not order him corporal punishment.

Thrapston Union Workhouse (later District Council Offices)

THE MENDICITY OFFICER UNDER ATTACK AGAIN

In 1871, the Chief Constable of Northampton took John Marmont in front of the Mayor, to make a complaint against J. Parker, the Mendicity Officer.

Marmont: I am on crutches, having lost one leg while serving in the Army in India during the Mutiny. Last evening, I arrived in Northampton about ten o'clock, having walked from three miles the other side of Wellingborough. I inquired at the Police Station where I could obtain a lodging, and I was directed to the Mendicity Office. A policeman went with me to show me the way. On arriving there, Mr. Parker refused to admit me, and said I was drunk. The policeman said I was perfectly sober, but still Parker refused to admit me, and told me he would have admitted me if the policeman had not been with me. He told the constable he could take me to the Devil. The constable then returned with me to the Station-House, and an inspector accompanied me to the Union Workhouse where I obtained lodging for the night. While we were walking to the Union, Parker passed us. I am not a beggar. I am a coachmaker, and I can work at my trade. I am on my way to London, where I hope to get work. If I do not succeed, I shall try to get admission to Chelsea Hospital, as I have served twenty-five years in the Army. I think it very hard, in England, to have such difficulty in obtaining a night's shelter.

The Chief Constable told the Mayor: "I am continually having similar complaints, and Parker often tells the police that he will not take people in; and he always sends back very impertinent messages.

The Mayor gave instructions for a letter of complaint to be written to the Northampton Guardians. "We are continually having complaints about the conduct of Parker. Give this man two shillings out of the poor-box."

Four days later, a meeting of the Guardians examined Parker about his conduct; but the Mendicity Officer had been doing some research: "Marmont had worked for a Northampton coachmaker that day, and he was paid. He was seen walking towards Wellingborough, not from it. He drank in a public house, and he was unruly. I was in bed when he was brought to me. I smelt beer on Marmont's breath, accurately. He was drunk. He lost his leg in London - in an accident in a shop.

The Guardians were satisfied with Parker's conduct, and believed that the police were mis-using the Mendicity Office.

WORKHOUSE FUNERALS

Elizabeth Norton died at the age of 66 in Wellingborough Union Workhouse in November 1871. On a Saturday afternoon, six of her fellow paupers carried her coffin to the cemetery chapel on a hand bier. The service was read over it by a clergyman, and the coffin was then carried to the waiting grave.

The sexton had lengthy experience in lowering coffins into graves. As soon as he felt the weight, he said: "It's empty!" The Cemetery Keeper lifted one end, and agreed.

Two other funerals were taking place nearby, and mourners began a murmuring that grew into a sensation. The officiating clergyman did his best to calm everyone. The coffin was opened and all could see that it was empty.

The Guardians heard the explanation at their next meeting: "It appears to be the practice for builders in the town alternately to supply the coffins for the Union. The present undertaker sent his man with the coffin to the mortuary where the deceased was lying in a shell, but he did not place the corpse in the coffin. As the time drew near for the funeral, the porter, supposing the body to be inside the coffin, ordered it to be screwed down and conveyed to the cemetery. Fortunately they were not far into the service when it was detected. They returned for the body, which was then interred in the presence of the relatives."

The practice of Thrapston Guardians was to invite tenders for the supply of coffins for a year at a time. They had to be taken, when required, to any of the twenty-six parishes of the Union.

An undertaker at Irchester wrote a letter to the Wellingborough Guardians:

I write to bring before your notice... the condition of the pall used at a parish [Union] funeral at Irchester... as it was not fit to be sent out in the state it was, as the stench from it was so great that the mourners and bearers with myself were quite overcome from it, and it was with great difficulty that the bearers could discharge their duty. It appears to have been used for some very bad cases, and then shut up in a box, or some other confined place, until wanted again, without airing... and I was also requested to ask you if you could use your influence towards the officiating clergymen being more punctual to time, as the time stated for this particular funeral was five o'clock. He then altered it to a quarter past six, and at that time we attended the churchyard gate with the corpse, but was compelled to wait twenty minutes before the reverend gentleman arrived, which was very hurtful to some and annoying to others...

The Guardians looked at this letter in August 1878, but their comments were impatient, and lacking in sympathy.

A correspondent to a weekly newspaper(19) in 1882 witnessed a funeral at Rushden. "The corpse was brought in a hearse from the Wellingborough Workhouse, and when it arrived at the Church gates at half past four, there were four men in their working clothes to carry it to the Church... When the corpse was at the grave and was being placed in, it was discovered that the grave was too short, so the coffin was again taken to the Church, and the grave was enlarged. The deceased was Abraham Ball, but the only inscription on the coffin was 'A.B. aged 60'."

The Wellingborough Local Board of Health, took the Guardians to task over the non-burial of a ten-month-old baby in 1884. The infant died at a lodging house, and lay unburied for many days because its parents could not afford a funeral. It had no coffin for four days, and the case was reported as a health nuisance. The Health Inspector went to the Relieving Officer, who stated that the parish was not liable for the child's burial. A private subscription was eventually raised to cover the cost, but the Health Board referred the case to the Guardians. A statement emerged: "The law is clear on the point. In cases of non-paupers the onus of burying the body lies with the householder where the lodger died."

An elderly woman died in the Daventry Workhouse in 1889. The Master sent the usual notice to the relatives:

"DAVENTRY UNION. Notice of Death.

21st August 1889. From the Master of the Workhouse to

Mrs. Jos. Mitchell.

I beg to inform you that Mary Tilley died this morning. If you have any requests to make respecting the funeral, please inform me on or before two o'clock to-morrow; otherwise it will take place on Friday next, at Long Buckby, at 2.30 p.m.

JOHN DAWE, Master."

The relatives travelled from Northampton to Long Buckby on the appointed day, and were at the churchyard at the stated time. The clergyman and the four bearers were also ready, but no coffin arrived. After waiting for an hour and ten minutes, the church was closed, and the clergyman and bearers went home. The son of the deceased went to the Telegraph Office to send a telegram to the Workhouse Master, but while he was there, a telegram arrived for the clergyman: "Reply paid, Rev. --- James, Long Buckby. Mistake in Tilley's funeral. Will Saturday do? Dawe." The Minister wired back: "Yes".

Nowhere was there any mention of the gross inconvenience caused to the deceased pauper's family.

THE TYPE OF NURSE WE WANT

The Wellingborough Guardians had before them a letter of resignation from Sarah Craddock, in November 1879. The reason she was giving up her situation as nurse at the workhouse, was that the work was too much for her.

A Guardian: She is too much of a lady. What we want is a powerful, strong, working woman, with a kind heart.

The Board decided to advertise for a nurse at a salary of £25 per annum.

A "CLIMBING BOY"

Anyone who has read Charles Kingsley's "The Water Babies" (or seen the film) knows of the early nineteenth century scandal of "climbing boys", the little boys employed by chimney sweeps to crawl up the old twisted chimneys. Acts of Parliament promoted by the 7th Earl of Shaftesbury in 1840 and 1864, intended to prohibit the use of boys, were disregarded by sweeps. Finally an Act of 1875 required chimney sweeps to be licensed, so that most sweeps began to take heed of the earlier laws, for fear of losing their licences.

In June 1880, Charles Barker, a Rushden chimney sweep, his face black with soot, stood before the Wellingborough Magistrates, charged with a breach of the Chimney Sweeps' Act by allowing a boy to climb a chimney.

Barker: I ask you, gentlemen, to excuse me for coming before you in this state, as I have not had time to wash myself. I wish to plead guilty to the charge. The boy who went up the chimney is thirteen years old, and he was apprenticed to me from the Workhouse, on the understanding that I should teach him all the branches of the business. In order to do so, I thought it necessary that the boy should climb the chimney. There are some chimneys that cannot be swept properly unless someone climbs them. I allowed the boy to climb the chimney on my own responsibility, knowing that it was rather against the law, but at the same time, I wanted the boy to thoroughly understand the business he was apprenticed to. No chimney sweep thoroughly learned his business without doing what I am now charged with.

The Chairman knew enough of the law to spot a flaw in the sweep's defence: "You appear to have acted under a misapprehension. The boy, you have told us, was apprenticed to you from the Workhouse, but a boy under sixteen years of age cannot be legally apprenticed to a chimney sweep".

Barker: Those at the Workhouse ought to have known that, as well as me. They sent him to me on the understanding that I was to teach him my trade in all its branches. I hope you will be as lenient with me as you possibly can.

Chairman: If difficulties arise in your business, you must overcome them by legal means. You knew you were transgressing the law when you sent the boy up the chimney.

Barker: I could have brought a character with me from several gentlemen, if I had thought of it.

Chairman: If you are ever brought before the Bench again, you will be severely dealt with. In the present case, you will be fined five shillings, and pay nine shillings and sixpence costs.

It was not all bad news for the sweep. A further charge, ill-treating the apprentice, was withdrawn, because as the Chairman had observed, the boy had not been legally bound to the sweep (20)

THE REAL "CHRISTMAS DAY IN THE WORKHOUSE"

"The inmates of the Workhouse were all very happy on Christmas Day, with the exception of two men. All but these two were plentifully supplied with roast beef and plum pudding, followed by dessert. Tobacco was distributed among the men, and snuff was given to the old women." This is the beginning of an account of Christmas Day at Wellingborough Union Workhouse in 1880.*(21)* We shall see shortly, the reason for the misery of the two excluded men.

"The dining halls were prettily decorated, and mirth and merriment prevailed, the whole of the day". Named benefactors had sent in "a collection of beautiful books", a box of oranges, the tobacco and snuff mentioned above, "a quantity of sweets" including a packet for each child, and a Christmas card for every inmate. "We forgot to ask the Master whether the two unhappy men got a card or not".

The two men who did not enjoy themselves at the Workhouse on Christmas Day were, of course, the individuals who applied for admission at the Guardians' meeting" of the previous week, "just for the sake of the extra fare they supposed they would get. They had been at that game before, but on this occasion, it did not succeed. The Board allowed them to enter the Workhouse, but gave instructions that only ordinary fare should be supplied to them on Christmas Day, and these instructions the Master faithfully carried out. He ordered the disreputable characters into the dining hall immediately before the feast, and one of them went, and ate bread and cheese, whilst the others partook of prime joints of beef. The second man proved refractory, and refused to enter the dining hall, and so he was left out in the cold, and had nothing at all to eat."

Eight years later, the writer, Marianne Farningham distributed the Christmas gifts that the public had contributed for the Workhouse children at Northampton. Within four days she was describing the occasion in the Northampton press: "At the Workhouse the toys had been set out in the Board-room, and delighted the eyes of the little company, who, having feasted on roast beef and plum pudding, were in good spirit for the occasion. The steam engine... I held before the admiring eyes of the boys, and asked any boy who would like it, to hold up his hand. Of course, all hands were shot up, and they are all going to have it, for that is for the use, or pleasure, of the Institution. The dolls, and books, and toys of all sorts were most gladly and gratefully accepted.

"There was only one thing I should like to see altered, and that is the girls' sleeves. Short sleeves are so cold. Few girls wear them now, and why they, more than the boys, ever should, I do not know. Long sleeves are much more comfortable. May not the next new winter-dresses have long sleeves?"

In 1891 the same House was "prettily decorated". In the men's dining room, "Ye roast beef of Old England" was written in large white letters on a blue background. 79 men sat down to the meal, and the Chairman of the Board, and three other Guardians performed as carvers. In the women's room, two other Guardians carved for the 28 women and 11 children. The women's nursery was decorated with holly, mottoes, and bannerettes. In there, another Guardian carved for the 19 women. Town Councillors carved in the females' infirmary (39 inmates). Another 13 inmates ate in the Old Women's Ward. The school room was "very prettily decorated"; 49 boys and 32 girls had their dinner in there.

Breakfast, served at half-past seven, was bread-and-butter and coffee. The dinner was roast beef, baked potatoes, and plum pudding, with half a pint of beer for each adult. At five o'clock, all 294 inmates were again served with bread-and-butter and coffee. During the evening, there was beer for the adults: a pint each for the men, and half a pint for the women. During the day, every child was given an orange. Tobacco was available for any adult smoker. After supper, the men and women, in their separate rooms were entertained by singers from among themselves. Before retiring, at ten, they gave hearty cheers for the staff of the House, and sang the National Anthem.

Ten miles away at Wellingborough, the House had been (Yes) "prettily decorated" under the guidance of the Master's wife. All unnecessary work was suspended, and the inmates left "to do pretty well as they liked". For dinner there was as much roast beef and plum pudding as they could eat, with coffee to follow. After that, snuff and tobacco for the elders, and nuts, oranges, dates, and sweets for all. A large assortment of toys had been sent in by benefactors. For tea: bread-and-butter and cake. Songs and recitations passed the evening away.

The descriptions and phrases are those of the local press.

GUARDIANS OBSERVED, 1881

W. W. Hadley was a 15-year-old apprentice reporter on a Northampton paper in 1881, and was assigned to attend a meeting of a Board of Guardians. He rose to be Editor of the Sunday Times. Seventy-six years later, he recalled that assignment. *(22)*

"For Boards of Guardians, there was plural voting and no ballot. Voting papers were left at the electors' houses and collected a day or two later. For Guardians, who existed to save the very poor from starvation, voters with the highest rateable value could give as many as twelve votes.

"The Boards of Guardians were often given a bad name, and it was a trying ordeal for any indigent person to appear before even the most considerate of them. Here is a stray memory of the Towcester Board, over seventy years ago. A timid little woman was shown into the room and stood facing the chairman, a good-natured farmer... When he asked what she wanted, she bobbed [a curtsey] and said in a low voice, 'I've come to see the Board, sir." He glanced round the room with a grin, and replied, 'Well, look at it, then!' There was a roar of laughter, but what amused the members frightened the poor creature who had come for their help. The old Duke of Grafton, who sat at one end of the long table, saw nothing to laugh at.

"Applications for relief were not reported in the papers."

THOSE WHO REFUSED TO GO IN

There were many destitute families and individuals who simply decided that they would not go into the workhouse, usually to avoid the stigma. John Askham, the Wellingborough poet, has given one sad example.(23) It occurred in the severe winter of 1879-80, when soup kitchens were set up in his town for those suffering hardship. "A poor old man, Isaac ----, who was infirm and aged. turned with great reluctance towards the Workhouse, in a window of which was the following notice: 'It is hoped that only those in actual want will apply'. Isaac returned home, which was both foodless and fireless, and died soon after."

The Guardians in the same town were concerned about the proliferation of beggars, not that they imposed on the resources of the Board. It is interesting that the contemporary term used by beggars to describe themselves was "askers". A Guardian in holy orders told his colleagues in 1880 that people should be induced to abstain from relieving beggars. A lady's servant had given notice and left her employment, to marry an "asker", because he could earn five pounds per week, and never less than 25 shillings. "Suppose a beggar made up his mind to 'do' Wellingborough, and then go on to Northampton. Beggars know well enough which are the best towns to visit, and which are the houses where they are likely to get money or food. They tell each other how they get on, and the consequence is that an honest householder who relieves one beggar, is visited shortly afterwards by other beggars. Wellingborough has, at present, a good name among beggars. Two of the tribe were heard talking the other day about their 'business', and one told the other that there are several good houses down Midland Road, where he could get a 'b' good tuck-in and some money too. 'Doing' Wellingborough is a profitable day's work for a beggar. Then, if he decides to remain in town, he gives himself up to a little indulgence in drink. Seven or eight quarts of beer between three of the fraternity were disposed of, this week, in this town". He was referring to a case dealt with by Wellingborough Magistrates, earlier that same day. They sent Mary Nolan to prison for seven days for drunkenness. She had fallen in with a blind "asker" at a lodging house. He had been unusually successful, and entertained a few friends, including Mary Nolan, with that quantity of beer.

The story of "Jumbo" at Northampton was a slightly different example of a man carefully keeping out of the Workhouse. He had another alias -"Black Jack"- but his name was Webster. He was able to earn a few shillings, doing casual work for the London and North-Western

Railway, during 1884. He spent his earnings on food, beer and tobacco, and to save on rent, slept rough in a railway shed. The police had many complaints about him, and arrested him just before Christmas. He was charged with sleeping in an outhouse, without visible means of subsistence. He had nothing to say to the Magistrates, and he was sentenced "as a rogue and vagabond" to two months in prison.

A similar case in the same town in 1888, was that of Susannah Coles. She was found by a constable, and charged with sleeping in a closet, without visible means of support. In Court, looking "very miserable", with an eye and a hand bandaged, she wept and told the Bench that she was a widow, and had fallen behind with her rent in a nearby village, thus losing her home. She had been "walking" for many months. The Magistrates told her she ought to go into the Workhouse.

Susannah: No, I shall never go there.

They sent her to prison for a week.

Nearly a year later, a Northampton shoe-hand was in London, at the Thames Police Court. His appearance was "wretched". He had been found wandering with his children, Alice, aged nine, and George, aged seven, and like the foregoing cases, was charged with having no visible means of subsistence. The accused man said that he had been forced to leave the Northampton boot factory where he had worked for fifteen years because he had quarrelled with his workmates. He had tramped to London.

The police inspector told the Magistrates that the two children were too ill to attend. The girl had told him at five that morning that she had been walking all night, and she could not recollect when she had last slept in a bed. Her mother was dead. The Surgeon had found that the feet of both exhausted children were covered with blisters, and had sent them to the Infirmary on an ambulance cart. In this case, as in the others, there was no question of seeking necessary support if it meant entering the Workhouse.

WORKHOUSE WEDDINGS

When the Peterborough Guardians met in September 1886, their Clerk read a letter he had received:

"Dogsthorpe, Peterborough, Sept. 15

Sir, -I write to ask if you have in your Union a likely young woman who would do for a wife for me. I am 64 years of age, and I begin to feel lonely. She can have a good home and plenty to eat and drink. I am, Yours, William Few.

P.S. If you have the likeness of any one of them, and give me their names, I shall be glad. I have just come to live here from Skegness."

The Master said that a few weeks ago a man called at the Workhouse and asked if there was a girl of 22 there, suitable for a wife. One of the Guardians remarked that they had several nice girls in the Union, and a photographer should be hired.

The Board decided to take no notice of the application.

A report of this part of the business was printed in several newspapers, and a copy of one of them must have been lying around for nearly three years. The same Board received the following:

"Werrington, Okeapple Day, 1889.

"Gents i was looking at some old news papers last week and i see one about a man wanting a wife out of the Union. i do the same as i am an old batchelor and i hear there are plenty of women in the big house let me know as soon as you can if there is one as wants a good husband i do not care how old she is.when i see the chaps and gals in our village larfing and talking and gigling and plaing it makes me blud run cold and me a single chap let me know soon

JOHN MITCHELL"

The Master of the Workhouse was informed of the contents of that letter with a view to providing a spouse for the lonely bachelor.

There was a happy ending to a case heard by Northampton Magistrates in 1887. Georgina N----, a widow, was charged with leaving her child chargeable to the Northampton Poor Law Union.

Evidence against her was given by the Master of the Workhouse and a police detective. She was asked what she had to say.

Georgina: ...Arrangements have been made for me to be married at All Saints' Church this morning, and if I wasn't called to the dock, I should have been at the altar. The bridegroom is here.

The groom was called forward. He offered to pay the costs of leaving the child at the Workhouse, and undertook to look after the child if the Bench dismissed the case. Thirty shillings was paid, and the happy pair left Court together to go to Church.

MAKING THE TRAMPS WORK

By the mid-1880s it was normal for casual inmates to be given work to earn their keep, even for an over-night stay. At Kettering in 1886, a committee was appointed by the Guardians to make arrangements for the employment of casual paupers admitted to the Workhouse. The committee arranged for a quantity of unbroken granite to be conveyed to the Workhouse for the vagrants to break up. In all fairness, the committee also arranged for printed notices to be displayed at the entrance to the Workhouse, "so that their casual visitors might not be taken unawares". The Workhouse Master reported a distinct falling off in the number of vagrants taken in.

Charles Walker was taken before Brackley Magistrates on the same day that he refused to carry out his allotted task at the Workhouse.(24) The Master, Wade, said that he had been admitted to the casual ward, and was given the usual work: four pounds of unbeaten oakum to pick. As the men were going to their tasks that morning, Walker started to walk away, "but he had not completed his task, so I fetched him back. He had only picked one and a half pounds of oakum. He said he had done a day's work, and refused to do any more. He was abusive and made use of bad language." Walker was sent to prison for a month with hard labour.

In March 1890, the Chairman of the Northampton Guardians graphically reported to his Board the escape of an ingenious tramp from a cell at the Workhouse. He smashed with his sledgehammer through a nine-inch brick wall at one place, which did not lead to the outside. He made another hole in the wall, and putting his hand through, drew back the door bolt, and so coolly escaped his task. "No doubt he is now not very far off, laughing at the Board's arrangements". The Guardians who visited had found that the brick partitions between the tramps' cells had in places, been broken through, so the cells were not "solitary" as had been supposed. It was also noticed that the partition walls had grown thinner, and were hardly half their original thickness. The Guardians decided to strengthen the damaged walls with blue bricks and good cement.

A PUZZLING STATEMENT BY A WORKHOUSE GIRL

In August 1882, Rosannah Farrell gave herself up to the police at Leicester, confessing to the murder of her own child. She made a statement:

"I have been an inmate of the Penitents' Home. I previously lost my character through prostitution. I was born at Woodford near Thrapston. My parents are dead, and I lived with my sister, the wife of a shoe-rivetter, at Kettering, until they went to live in Northampton. I was in a bad house at Weedon, kept by a person called Little Nance. She was present at the birth of my child, a girl, born in 1879 or 1880. When the child was four months old, I drowned it. I walked from Weedon to Northampton and thence to Thrapston, carrying the baby. I was walking all day, and had nothing to eat, and about ten o'clock at night, I come to a bridge with three arches. I got over a wall, and put the child in the water and drowned it. I had intended going to my aunt who keeps a public house at Thrapston, but after I drowned my baby, my heart misgave me, and I went back to Northampton and stayed with my sister. The Vicar of All Saints' sent me to the Penitents' Home at Leicester in 1881.

I have continued to have a heavy weight on my mind, and I wish to make this confession. The baby was in good health at the time I drowned it."

The police took her before the Leicester Magistrates, but told them that enquiries seemed to discredit the girl's story.

She was remanded, pending further investigation. Five days later, an inspector of the Northamptonshire Constabulary told the Leicester Bench that, in company with a Leicester Superintendent, he had made enquiries in the district in which the crime was said to have been committed, but they had ascertained nothing to corroborate the Miss Farrell's statement.

"I have made further enquiries, and find that it is utterly impossible for the prisoner to have been confined at the time she stated. She was brought up in the Workhouse as a child, and the Master at the Thrapston Union told me that some three years ago, she was in the habit of hiding things and accusing herself of stealing them."

The Penitents' Home refused to take her back. She refused to go to any of her relatives, but the Leicester Union agreed to take her. The Leicester Magistrates discharged her to go into the Workhouse there. *(25)*

AN INSPECTOR CALLS

W. A. Peel, an inspector from Whitehall (The Local Government Board), visited the Union Workhouse at Kettering in October 1884, and attended the next meeting of the Board of Guardians to give his report:

Wootton Workhouse

"...The hospital wards are not only faulty in management, but are carelessly and insufficiently attended to, so that neither the comfort nor cleanliness of the patients can be properly assured. There is want of proper classification of the sick, and... sick persons are located in various parts of the House distinct from each other, make it impossible for the hospital nurse, however active and efficient she might be, properly looks after her charges... Opportunities for misappropriating the food and other necessaries for the sick, are almost unbounded... Existing buildings such as the carpenter's shop and store-room appear to be but little used, and could be adopted for hospital purposes... The condition of the boys' and men's sleeping and day rooms is unsatisfactory. I have seen articles of clothing lying on and under the beds at about two o'clock, the time I visited the Workhouse. Neither the Master of the House nor the porter are in the habit of visiting the different rooms as they are required to do... The dirty condition of several of the men who were in the yard led me to inquire into the matter of lavatory accommodation, and I found on examination, that things were radically wrong, and the smells in the vicinity of the urinals and closets were unbearable."

The Master, John Moore, put his response in writing:

"...In respect to the dirty and untidy condition of the House... I am sorry to say that in two or three wards the sweeping had not been properly done, and there was dirt under some of the beds, and a pair of shoes under a bed in a room used as a sick ward. I have looked after the wardsmen myself every morning... The untidiness of the boys' play-room was caused by their having some old cord jackets and vests given them to wear in the morning and between school hours, to save their school clothes. When the boys were called to school, these were thrown off in a hurry, and left on the seats and table. This will not occur again, as the old clothes have been removed. The dirty appearance of the floor and yard is the result of the scarcity of water: we have not been able to wash the place thoroughly for nearly three weeks. As to visiting the wards, I am sorry to say that in consequence of severe rheumatism, I have not felt able at all times to visit all the wards, but the Matron has certainly been in almost all the wards once a day, and in many of them, twice. She has had all the wards scoured out at least once every week. Since Mr. Peel's visit, I have been through the wards at the proper times. Mr. Peel called attention to the particular case of an old man who had not been supplied with the ordinary house diet. He became ill and unable to take any regular diet, and the Medical Officer ordered the Matron to let him have milk, arrowroot, or beef-tea, whichever he should like best. That order was strictly carried out until the poor man's death. Hoping this explanation may be satisfactory to your honourable Board..."

MORE TROUBLE AT THE KETTERING WORKHOUSE

In January 1885, Charles Hodgkins, aged 14, absconded from the Kettering Workhouse, taking the clothes issued to him. He was brought back by the police, but reportedly not punished by the Master because he wished his case to be dealt with by the Guardians. The boy was taken before the Magistrates and sentenced to fourteen days with hard labour, in Northampton Gaol. The Governor of the Gaol reported to the Home Secretary that the boy's body was covered with weals and bruises, and that the boy accused the Master, John Moore, of flogging him.

At the Kettering Guardians' February meeting, the Local Government Board Inspector, Peel, was present. He had seen the Home Office papers on the case. Witnesses were called. The Master, a female caretaker, the Porter, and inmates gave evidence to the Guardians.

There were seventeen boys in the House, some of them "very bad" and violent. One small boy had constant black eyes. Corporal punishment was regular, with cane or rod. The Master admitted not making entries in the punishment book.

Within two weeks, the Guardians received Moore's letter of resignation from the Mastership, but did not accept it at that time. They asked Peel to investigate.

Another two weeks passed, and by that time, the Workhouse boys were in open revolt against the authority of the officers.

They smashed seventy panes of glass in the windows, on one Sunday evening. The Guardians accepted the resignation of the Moores (Master and Matron), but when they called an Inquiry, one faction of the Board put the blame on the boy Hodgkins. One Guardian described him as "the most incorrigible scamp within these islands". (The Guardian and the boy both came from Rothwell). "He inflicted mutilations on himself in order to bring a charge against the Rothwell schoolmaster; and I have myself have given him a whipping for stealing from my premises". Boy witnesses were called to give evidence. They were all very untidy and it was observed that they "reflected anything but credit upon those responsible for their appearance". The porter was accused of brutal treatment of the boys. He had struck one on the head with a key, causing him to bleed over his bed sheets.

A lame boy, Alfred Evans, aged 12, was called before the Guardians. He had broken some windows himself - because breakfast had been dry bread. The Porter, Simcoe, had thrashed him and others with a thick walking stick. He had first come into the Workhouse when his mother died, and Simcoe had beaten him then, "because I wasn't quick enough getting into bed".

Others testified as to the violence of Simcoe, and also of the Schoolmistress, Jane Birch. An adult male pauper had seen the Porter strike a boy with a big walking stick, "enough to knock his little thighs off". The Porter had not yet been interviewed. "He is drunk, now, up in the casual ward, swearing like a bulldog at two tramps", said the pauper. Simcoe was sent for. He shuffled into the room, "hiccoughing every few words he spoke" and answering in a "screeching key". He told the Inquiry that he could not manage the boys, and had no power over them. He had always been kind to them: "Oh dear, yes, always"; but he had been grossly insulted by them.

The Inquiry went into a second day. Grounds were agreed to dismiss Simcoe. Jane Birch, the Schoolmistress, was closely questioned. Her own problems caused her to hit the boys. They were insolent to her, frequently. She had often seen Simcoe drunk.

The Porter was called again. He described the bad behaviour of the boys, admitted "boxing their ears", but denied inflicting severe physical punishment. He was told that the Inquiry intended to recommend his dismissal because he was "not a fit person". He thereupon produced an envelope which, he said, contained his resignation; but it was refused because "It is too late, Simcoe".

At the end of the proceedings, Moore, the Master, asked for and was given, authorisation to have all the broken glass repaired, 170 panes in all.

At Kettering Police Court in April 1885, five boys, including Charles Hodgkins, were brought up, accused of assault on fellow inmates. An order was made to place Hodgkins in an Industrial School until he was sixteen. (He was not quite fourteen).

During April, advertisements were placed in the press for Master and Matron, and Porter and "Portress".

Was that the end of the disorder? A local newspaper reported on 25th April: "The boys continue to be in a state of anarchy, and have again broken a large number of panes in the windows during the week." A quantity of picked oakum stored in a back room was found to be on fire one morning. Incendiarism was considered unlikely. The cause was attributed to "a spark from the pipe of an adult pauper".

Moore was replaced as Master by Berry, and a year later, all seemed satisfactory.

On Friday, 7th May 1886, a tramp obtained an order for admission. He arrived in a filthy state, obviously ill. As he shuffled into the casual ward, scarcely able to put one foot in front of the other, Berry could see that he was suffering from an eruptive skin complaint, and decided to isolate him.

The man was placed in an unused part of the building, and Berry allowed no-one but himself to come into contact with him until he had been examined by the Medical Officer. Three days later, he was transferred to the Infectious Diseases Hospital in Kettering, and the room at the Workhouse in which he had slept was as thoroughly disinfected. Confluent Smallpox had been diagnosed. By Saturday 22nd May, Berry had Smallpox. He was isolated, and placed under proper care in an upper room, but his condition worsened, and in six days he was dead. There were attempts to keep the tragedy secret in the town, but rumours spread, and by the day of the Master's funeral, the story was well-known. The tramp, meanwhile, made excellent progress, and by June was convalescent. *(26)*

FAILED SUICIDE

Joseph D---- was admitted to the Workhouse Infirmary at Northampton in November 1885, suffering from several burns to the throat and mouth. He had obtained some gunpowder, and attempted suicide by the novel method of filling his mouth with it. He had to open his mouth to insert burning paper to ignite it, so sufficient resistance was not given to the explosive to have the desired effect. His condition was precarious for two days, but he recovered.

A BAD REPORT ON THRAPSTON WORKHOUSE

Inspector Peel visited Thrapston Union Workhouse on 27th June 1887. His report should have been under scrutiny by the Guardians in July, but the Chairman had [conveniently?] forgotten to bring it into their meeting. "I shall read extracts from my own notes on it", he explained. "Mr. Peel stated that he found it in a discreditable condition. On the male side of the House the beds were either unmade, or had been used since being made. Some of the bolsters in the dormitories were without straw. The earth closets were in an offensive state. Inmates and casuals cutting wood were employed together. That is contrary to the regulations. The male and female reception wards were in a filthy state, and littered with feathers. The infectious ward was foul, and in a disgraceful condition. The washerwomen complained that their beer had been withheld. The mortuary was disgraceful, and in it was a dead body not properly attended to. In the hospital was a sick lad lying in bed without sheets. The Nurse said that she had asked for the sheets but could not get any. The inmates said that the soup and beef-tea they were supplied with were unfit to drink, but - and I wish to call especial attention to this - they told the Inspector that they dare not complain, or they would suffer for it. Some days they have to go without food. On Friday the 24th of June, the Master was absent from the House without leave, from 9.26 a.m. to 9.30 p.m., and he gave an unsatisfactory reason for his absence. He remarked to the Inspector, that the House was a tumble-down old place, and he could not keep it in order. In 1883, our own visiting committee had called attention to the high cost of in-maintenance, being two shillings or more higher, per head, than in other unions. In 1886, our visiting committee reported the same, expressing their belief that the excess cost could be attributed to nothing other than bad management. The Inspector stated that he had frequently warned the Master that the present state of things must come to an end, and had given him every chance of improvement. The Inspector gave me the impression that if the Guardians do not get rid of the Master, the Local Government Board will intervene. We have, for some time, treated the Master with great indulgence, which has even approached the verge of weakness. It has been inevitable for a long time that a crisis must come."

The Guardians loudly applauded their Chairman. One of them stated that the actual report was in much stronger language.

Another Guardian considered that the inmates had suffered very greatly on account of the Master's large family. However, he pointed out that the visiting committee of Guardians had made 39 inspections in the last two years, and 38 times reported the Workhouse "satisfactory".

One Guardian had been keeping his own record of the Master's movements. "On the 1st of June, the Master left home at 10 a.m., and returned at 5.30; left again at 7 o'clock, and had not returned by 10.30 p.m. On the evening of June 21st, the Master did not return to the House to see if the inmates had safely come back from the Jubilee celebration." (The whole country was celebrating Queen Victoria's Silver Jubilee) "On June 23rd, the Master went out by the 9.30 train, and did not return until late at night. He went to a public-house, and had not come back to the House at ten o'clock. Friday, the next day, was the absence mentioned in the Inspector's report".

Before the end of this meeting, the Master entered and placed an envelope in the hands of the Chairman. Inside was a letter:

"Union House, Thrapston.

"July 12th, 1887.

"Gentlemen, -By Order of the Board, we beg to resign our appointments as Master and Matron to this Workhouse... Trusting we may leave the House as clean and in good order as we found it sixteen years ago... R. J. Wakefield and Louisa Ellen Wakefield".

TRADES OF KETTERING VAGRANTS

Vagrants taking casual beds at the Kettering Union Workhouse during 1887 were required to give their trades. Many were, of course, labourers, but there were also cabinet-makers, carpenters, watchmakers, grocers, clerks, surveyors, barbers, musicians, and a lion-tamer.

FIRE-DRILL AT THE ASYLUM

Mentally unfit inmates from all the workhouses were placed in the County Asylum. In Northamptonshire, this was a short distance to the west of Northampton, at Berry Wood.

In April 1888, Guardians visiting the asylum to report on the condition of patients from their own unions were privileged to see a firedrill. There were impressive appliances to be seen. Dr. Green gave the signal by blowing a whistle, and in two minutes, the fire escapes were out. A man on horseback was ready to ride to Northampton for additional help. A line of girls appeared, with buckets, standing ready to serve the manual engine.

APRIL FOOL!

A family in Irchester village proudly announced the birth of a baby girl. "The mother and child progressed very satisfactorily, and the father was as proud of his first-born as young fathers generally are". The mother was seen to caress the babe frequently, and the father loved to dandle her on his knee. On Saturday, 16th June 1888, the family was among a party of friends. The young mother had some startling information for the father, which she gave out in public, for all to hear. The child was not his. She had never given birth to a child. Nearly three months earlier, the father's "firstborn" had been "fetched from the Workhouse". His wife had played an incredible trick on him. The husband was observed to be unwilling to accept the truth of the revelation for a while, "but the evidence was so strong that he had to admit that he had been imposed upon." (27)

MEDICAL OFFICERS

In every district of a union, a doctor was appointed to be Medical Officer. He usually had his own practice, but his

Poor Law appointment gave him a salary, for which he was expected to treat patients in the Workhouse. When given authorisation by the Relieving Officer or a Guardian, he was also expected to deal with illness or injuries among the poor in his own district.

In 1884, the Wellingborough Board of Guardians requested the Medical Officer of their Wollaston District, Dr. Orr, to attend their October meeting. They wanted him to explain the treatment of a boy who had crushed his hand in a machine. Dr. Orr had been absent on holiday, and one of the Guardians had ordered the boy to be taken to his locum. The hand had been bound up, but two days later, the boy went for more treatment. This time, the locum cut off one finger, and sent him to the Northampton Infirmary. The boy's mother alleged that, at the Infirmary, the surgeon said that the boy ought to have been brought there immediately after the accident, and hesitated to admit him. She said that the finger had been hanging by a piece of skin.

The Guardians were reluctant to pay the medical fee to Dr. Orr. Their Clerk told them that a Guardian had no right to order treatment. Overseers or Churchwardens had that duty, and the Auditor would not sanction the fee.

Dr. Orr: My locum tenens has an extensive Union practice, and he is a thoroughly qualified practitioner. He reported the case to me on my return home. It is a proper case for the extra fee. Unfortunately the gentleman is now on the way to Egypt. [General Gordon was besieged in the Sudan, and the Guardians were, no doubt, meant to be impressed by the locum's destination]

Dr. Orr had exchanged letters with the House Surgeon at Northampton Infirmary, who said that the mother herself had looked after the boy's hand too long before seeking medical advice. "My opinion", said Dr. Orr, "is that conservative surgery was correct. Amputation as a last resort could have been done at a later time, if necessary. My locum appears to have made an effort to save the finger, but finding, on the boy's second visit, that this was impossible, he amputated the worst part, and sent him on to Northampton Infirmary". The doctor was asked to retire from the meeting, and the Guardians had a lengthy discussion, and concluded that Dr. Orr's locum tenens had acted to the best of his judgment, but the Board was unable to pay the fee, which would be disallowed by the Auditor.

At the time of the foregoing incident, a professional controversy was raging in the Oundle Union, concerning the administration of medical relief in the Weldon district. The Oundle Guardians appointed a Medical Officer at Weldon in 1880 who was not on the register of medical practitioners. Another doctor in that village, Stokes, protested repeatedly to the Board of Guardians, but the unregistered man was still the Medical Officer three years later. It is not clear whether he had been struck off, or if there was another reason why he was unable or unwilling to produce any certificate of qualification. In 1883, his name was restored to the register, but he resigned and went abroad. The aggrieved Dr. Stokes was then appointed, but discovered that his salary was ten pounds less than that of his unregistered predecessor. He resigned, and the nearest replacement for him was a resident in another village eight miles away. However, Dr. Stokes found himself being called to all emergencies that occurred in Weldon, because he was there, and the Medical Officer was not. There was no prospect of any payment for attending these emergencies, so Dr. Stokes swallowed his pride and offered to take on the appointment of Medical Officer at the reduced salary. The Guardians declined the offer, so Dr. Stokes complained to his professional association. *(28)*

An appeal was made to the Local Government Board in Whitehall, but in deference to the wishes of the Oundle Guardians, the non-resident doctor was confirmed in his appointment.

The enraged Dr. Stokes, almost immediately, was called upon to attend to two very urgent cases in Weldon, requiring the prompt and immediate attention that the Medical Officer, eight miles away was unable to provide.

TOWCESTER WORKHOUSE INSPECTED

Henry Howard Packer, the Master of the Union Workhouse at Towcester, allocated tasks to the male inmates on the morning of 15th October 1888. William Wake and Joseph Holloway were given half a ton of stone to break up. At the end of the day, they had managed to crack only four hundredweight, less than half of it. The Master knew "plenty of men that could break two tons in a day". Those were his words given in evidence in Court, when the Clerk to the Board of Guardians took the two work-shy paupers before the Magistrates. The Clerk told the Bench that the two were constantly coming in and out of the Workhouse, and the amount of labour they were expected to accomplish was explained to them, and understood, when they were admitted. Wake told the Magistrates that he was 67 years old. Not true: he was 57. Perhaps that was the reason he was sentenced to ten days' imprisonment with hard labour, and his friend Holloway only seven days.

About this time, Mr. Peel, was at the Workhouse to carry out his inspection for the Local Government Board. He attended the Guardians' meeting in person, to give them his report.

The Master had told him that men were sleeping in the "cells" in twos, which was against the law. "The answer to that," said a Guardian, "is the stone-breaking." He meant that the need for doubling-up was less, because the stone-breaking task deterred men from coming into the House. "But a difficulty was caused when the railway work first commenced, and men in a destitute condition came into the town." That was not the Great Central, which came through that district during the next decade. The Guardian was referring to the building of the Towcester and Olney line, which had commenced during the year. The project evidently attracted unemployed men, who desired to sleep in the Workhouse. So sometimes two had to go in a cell.

Inspector: There should be some alteration effected in the accommodation for the sick. I found every bed occupied in the male sick ward, and in the women's sick ward, I found nine persons sitting in a room intended for six. The other three were supposed to sleep in another room, but I was told that they did not stop there, because there was no fireplace. The difficulty might be removed by a rearrangement of the rooms.

Mr. Peel also complained that inmates were provided with only two blankets - "and very thin ones, too". Almost every other workhouse allowed three blankets.

"I understand that the men are all made to go to bed in the dark, and last night a youth, who has only one leg, tumbled over, and his crutch went through a window."

The Guardians roared with laughter.

"There is another matter. I do not consider that it is quite right to put a woman who has an illegitimate in charge of girls. I think some other person should be found. Now let me refer to the dietary arrangements. This is the only Workhouse where the old people - old, infirm people, over sixty years of age - get dry bread for their breakfast. Most people over sixty in other Houses, have tea, and butter on their bread.

The Master, Henry Packer, was called into the room, and asked to explain why the men went to bed in the dark. "Candles are used in the sick wards, but there is no light on the stairs, nor in the rooms. The men retire to bed early, before dusk, so lights are not deemed to be necessary."

Inspector: The non-use of lights is contrary to the law.

Master: I always carry a light through the rooms after the men have retired.

Inspector: I must point out, the law demands that a light should be used on the inmates retiring to rest.

When the Towcester Guardians met next month, November 1988, they heard details of the action taken on the Inspector's report:

1. Men would occupy a cell each, except occasionally in the spring and autumn, when tramps in large numbers passed through, on their way to and from the fruit and hop picking in the south.

2. Numbers would be eased in the women's infirm ward, by moving some into "lying-in ward".

3. The Master had been directed to place a candle at the door of the men's ward at bed-time.

4. Three blankets were normally provided, but owing to the warm weather, had not been asked for. The extra one would be supplied at once.

5. There was not woman in the House, capable of supervising the children, who had not had an illegitimate child!

6. The aged people of both sexes each had a pint of tea, morning and evening, and had done so for many years. At that present time, the men had cheese in the evening, and the woman had butter. Details of the breakfasts, dinners, and suppers provided at Towcester Union were compared with those provided at Northampton Union. The figures said that Towcester inmates were better fed.

A PAUPER'S HAT

On 4th May 1889, an old man died in the Workhouse at Wellingborough. King Darnell - that was the name in the register - was known for the billycock hat he always wore. He showed an extraordinary affection for it, and even during his final illness, he refused to let it be taken away from him. When they were laying him out, and his apparel was removed, the hat was found to be unusually weighty. The "billy" was examined, and in the lining was found a large number of coins, to the value of twelve shillings and sixpence. Eleven shillings of it was in pennies and halfpennies. When the treasure was handed over to the

Master, Simmons, he entered the amount in his current expenses book. *(29)*

HELPFUL STATISTICS FOR THE BRACKLEY GUARDIANS

William Page, of the village of Moreton Pinkney, worked on the roads for many years, usually breaking stones. The time came when his advanced age and his medical condition made retirement necessary. He had been subject to fits for several years. He realised that he was likely to end his days in the Workhouse, and on Wednesday, 21st August 1889, he joined the line of applicants to go before the Brackley Guardians. When his turn came, he placed in front of them a record he had kept of all the fits he had suffered during the previous ten years. In 1879, there had been 44. In 1880, 78. In 1881, 121. 196 in 1882. 559 fits in 1883. In 1884: 435. 273 in 1885, and only 251 in 1886. An increase to 447 in 1887, and 600 in 1888. The total number of methodically recorded fits was 3,004.

The Guardians were impressed. Several had seen him lying on the roadside in a fit. One of them had seen him lying at the verge, in a fit, with a scythe in his hand. Instead of ordering him into the House, they granted him three shillings and threepence per week. *(30)*

AN ORDER FOR THE HOUSE

An elderly couple at Wellingborough in 1897, who had been on outdoor relief for some time, were served with an "order for the House". The minutes of their interview with the

Board of Guardians explains why the treatment of their case changed.

Before they were brought into the room, the Relieving Officer told the Guardians what he knew: "According to the woman's account, she has had to leave her husband, and they now live apart. She stated that when she left, she took £2 with her, and left him with about £20. They have been receiving three shillings a week each, in relief from the Union."

The Guardians decided to question her. She confirmed that she had taken £2 and left home.

Chairman: How much did you leave behind?

Woman: About £20, I think.

Chairman: How is that you want this six shillings a week relief, then? You have no business to have it. You and your husband have been taking relief together, while you have all this money in your house; and it's not fair to the ratepayers.

Woman: I hadn't been married six weeks before he punched me in the eye. [She placed her own fist in her eye]

Chairman: Are you his second wife?

Woman: I'm his third. [Sensation around the table]

Chairman: Any children?

Woman: No, sir.

Relieving Officer: You came to me for relief, while you had that £2, and I gave you an order for the House.

Chairman: What business had you, to go to him, with that in your possession?

The woman did not answer. She was dismissed, and the husband was brought in. The Guardians were surprised to see in front of them, "a decrepit old man".

Chairman: We understand that your wife has left you.

Man: Yes, but what is the reason, I can't tell you. On Tuesday morning seven weeks yesterday, I called her to come downstairs, and she had her breakfast. Then she began shifting things. I didn't know till then that she'd been working things out of the house.

Chairman: Did she "work" some money out of the house?

Man: Yes.

Chairman: How much?

Man: I don't know.

Chairman: Do you think - as much as £2?

Man: I don't know.

Chairman: How did she come to have £2, when she left you?

Man (confidingly): Well, it's my opinion she must have a good bit of money. As soon as ever I got in from my hawking, I gave her every penny I had took, even before I had a drink of tea.

Chairman: She took care of the money, then?

Man: Yes, and I never knowed anything. She never told me she had money in the bank. She told me afterwards that she had it when her second husband died.

Chairman: How much did she leave you in the house, when she went?

Man: I found eight shillings in my pocket.

Chairman: Did you find twenty pounds?

Man: No. I wish I could've.

A Guardian: Where did you keep your money?

Man: I never had none from her.

Guardian: Where did she keep it, then?

Man: She never told me.

Guardian: Did you quarrel about money?

Man: We never quarrelled about anything.

Chairman: What made her go away?

Man: Ah! That's what the neighbours want to know. (Laughter)

Chairman: What did she take out of the house?

Man: She took her clothes, and everything off the bed in the garret - the pillows, sheets and blankets an' all.

Chairman: Have you got any money?

Man: No, I'm not got any money. Yes, I am, though. I won't tell you a lie.

He laid one penny on the table, theatrically, in front of the Chairman.

Chairman: You'll lose it, if you don't mind it.

Relieving Officer: He told me himself, that his wife took £3.

The woman was called back in.

Chairman: As a married woman living apart from your husband, you cannot continue on outdoor relief, and you will have an order for the House. You have money in the bank, though.

Woman: Yes, but it's all gone.

A Guardian: Where does your husband keep his money?

Woman: In his box. He had £9 when he married me. I don't know where he got it from.

Chairman: You were the one who kept the money, weren't you?

Woman: No.

Chairman: Where is the bag?

Woman: In his box.

There was some discussion by the Board, and then the old man was brought back in.

Chairman: The Board has resolved not to give you any more relief, and you will have an order for the House. We are not satisfied with what we have heard about the arrangements between you and your wife. If you can keep out of the House, so much the better.

The old man began mumbling incoherently: "...a little bit of ground..."

PERSONS, NOT PAUPERS

The Wellingborough Guardians, on 8th April 1896, heard their Clerk read a letter from the local Secretary of the National Union of Boot and Shoe Workers. "Several Boards of Guardians", it said, "have been successful in establishing the word 'person' in place of 'pauper' in all official documents. We desire that your Board should do the same, and drop a word which is becoming a sort of byword..."

This request would have seemed quite normal exactly a century later, at a time when all public utterances were expected to be "politically correct", and words that had once been in common use, such as "cripple", "blind" and "short" were unacceptable, and needed to be substituted by socially-approved euphemisms: "disabled", "visually-handicapped" and "dimensionally-challenged".

The Wellingborough Board, which by 1896 had a woman-member, did not, apparently consider the request in any way strange.

The Rev. M. E. Parkin proposed that the suggestion be adopted.

Mr. P. Dulley: If this resolution is carried, what will happen to any member of the Board who says the word "pauper"? (Laughter)

Mrs. Lloyd Pratt: They will have to apologise. (Laughter) The contents of the letter are exactly my sentiments, and I will second the motion.

It was carried unanimously.

7. When the Workhouses Came to an End

The Workhouse regime was essentially a feature of the Victorian age. From the very start of the twentieth century, a new philosophy began to develop in the administrative treatment of poverty. During the South African War, an alarming proportion of the men volunteering for military service had to be rejected on the grounds of ill-health and malnutrition. This led directly to legislation in 1907 authorising local councils to provide free meals for needy children. This was the first of a series of administrative measures which created the "Welfare State".

In 1908 Old-Age Pensions removed the fear of ending one's days in the Workhouse. Anyone over 70, with an income of less than £21 a year, became entitled to an allowance of five shillings a week. In 1909, Labour Exchanges ("Job Centres") were set up to facilitate the re-employment of the unemployed.

National Insurance, a scheme copied from the Germans in 1911, provided workers with security against unemployment and ill health.

Responsibility for the relief of poverty was taken from the Local Government Board in 1919, and given to the newly created Ministry of Health: a major step in the dismantling of the Victorian structure. The completion of the process was part of Neville Chamberlain's Local Government Act of 1929. The 642 Boards of Guardians were abolished at a stroke. Their functions were given to County Councils and County-Borough Councils. They were required to have public assistance committees - and the workhouses became "public assistance institutions".

REFERENCES

1. Assize Roll 817 (1203) IN D. M. Stenton: The Earliest Northamptonshire Assize Rolls. 1930. (NRS)

2. PRO: Ancient Correspondence Vol. I, No. 66. Trans. by R. M. Serjeantson. IN Journal of Northamptonshire Natural History Society Vol. XVI 1911-12 p. 226.

3. State Papers Domestic 12/81/14 (1571) quoted, Joan M. Wake. The Brudenells of Denne. 1953. (Cassell)

4. Sternberg: Dictionary of Northamptonshire Fold Lore...1851. 5. J. Charles Cox, ed. Records of the Borough of Northampton Vol. II. 1898.

6. Ibid

7. Earls Barton Parish Chest (transcribed into a ledger)

8. NRO: ZA 211/1 Dorothy Hensman, Account Book, 1816.

9. NRO: 285P 283 p.14 J. Enos Smith, transcription from original, 1910.

10. Northamptonshire Notes and Queries Vol. I No. 102. 1884. (from Sheffield collection, Earls Barton)

11. Northampton Mercury 14 March 1829.

12. Commissioners on the Poor Laws, 1st Report. 1834. Appendix A, pp. 397-417, No. 14: Northamptonshire.

13. Northampton Mercury 15 July 1837.

14. Poor Law Commission, Second Annual Report, 1836.

15. Northampton Mercury 2 December 1837.

16. Inspector of Prisons for the Southern and Western District, Seventh Report (Northamptonshire) 1842.

17. Northampton Mercury 21 April 1838.

18. Northampton Mercury 26 December 1846.

19. Wellingborough and Kettering News 27 May 1882.

20. Rushden and District History Society Newsletter, 1996.

21. Wellingborough and Kettering News 1 January 1881.

22. W. W. Hadley: Northamptonshire Memories II, IN Northamptonshire Past and Present Vol. II, No. 4. 1957. p.175.

23. John Askham. Sketches in Prose and verse. 1893.

24. Brackley Observed Vol. I, No. 3. 1989, p.30.

25. Wellingborough and Kettering News 12 August 1882.

26. Kettering Observer 4 June 1886.

27. Northampton Mercury 23 June 1888.

28. British Medical Journal, December 1885.

29. Northampton Mercury 18 May 1889.

30. Northampton Mercury 24 August 1889.